# TICKET
## DIARY
# STUB

*Jayme* | Books
DESIGN

**A BIG THANK YOU FOR SUPPORTING INDEPENDANT PUBLISHING**
**WE HOPE YOU ARE HAPPY WITH YOUR PURCHASE**

Why not Subscribe to our once a month newsletter
We promise it to be spam free and contain only fun and informative
news and updates on all our latest release and Editor monthly
recommendations.

**SIMPLY SCAN THE QR CODE BELOW**

---

## REVIEWS ARE IMPORTANT! ★★★★★

Your feedback and comments are greatly appreciated
on Facebook and Amazon. Both help us bring the best to you
and our customers. A few seconds of your valuable time would mean
a huge difference to helping us maintain quality standards
Thank you!

**WHY NOT FIND, FOLLOW AND LIKE US ON FACEBOOK!**
Comments, question and reviews are always welcome

---

# TICKET
DIARY
# STUB

**DATE:**

**MY MEMORIES**

# TICKET
DIARY
# STUB

**DATE:**

**MY MEMORIES**

# TICKET
DIARY
# STUB

**DATE:**

## MY MEMORIES

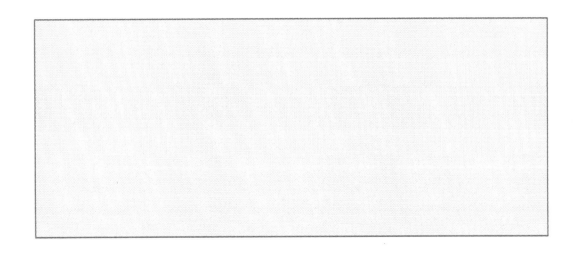

# TICKET
DIARY
# STUB

**DATE:**

**MY MEMORIES**

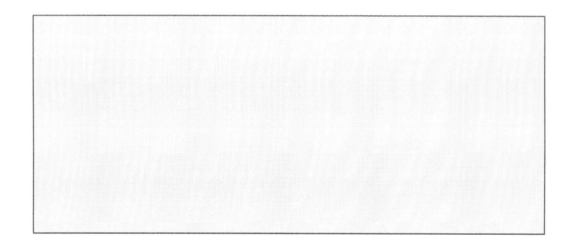

# TICKET
DIARY
# STUB

**DATE:**

**MY MEMORIES**

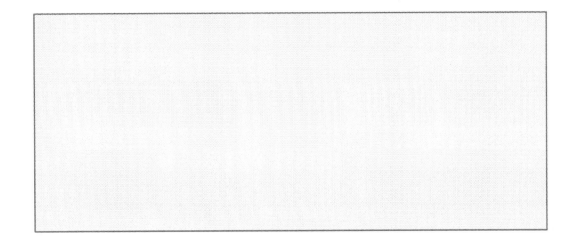

# TICKET
DIARY
## STUB

**DATE:**

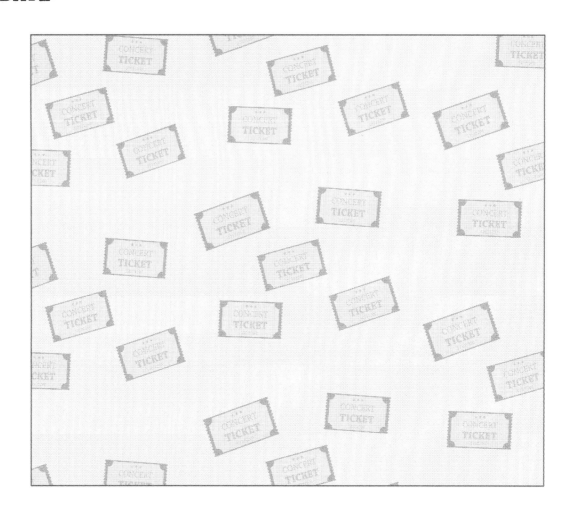

**MY MEMORIES**

# TICKET
DIARY
# STUB

**DATE:**

**MY MEMORIES**

# TICKET
DIARY
## STUB

**DATE:**

## MY MEMORIES

# TICKET
### DIARY
## STUB

**DATE:**

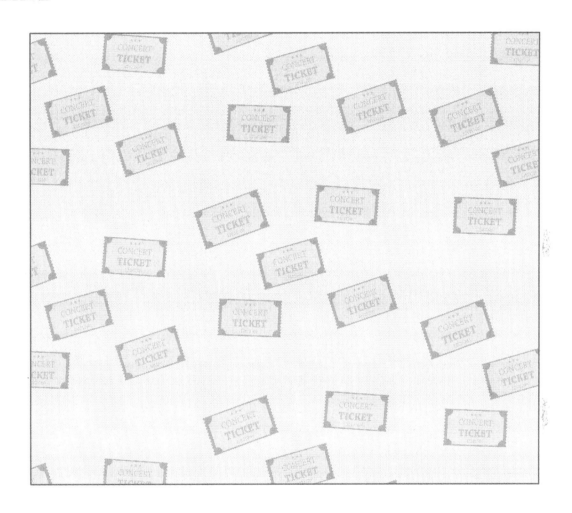

## MY MEMORIES

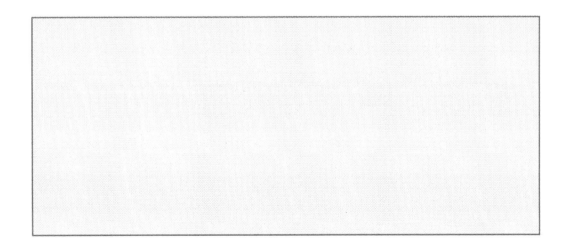

# TICKET
DIARY
## STUB

**DATE:**

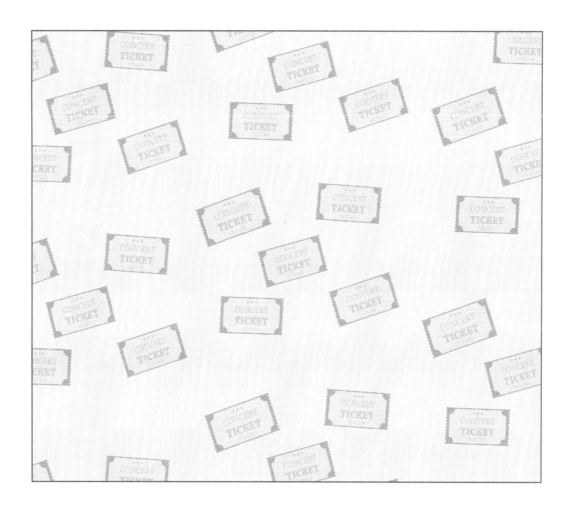

## MY MEMORIES

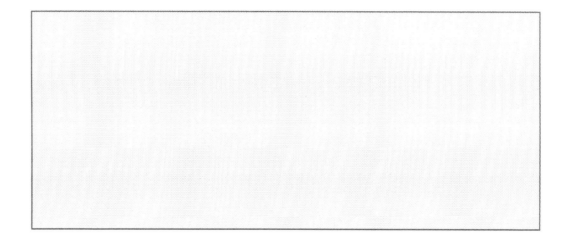

# TICKET
DIARY
# STUB

**DATE:**

**MY MEMORIES**

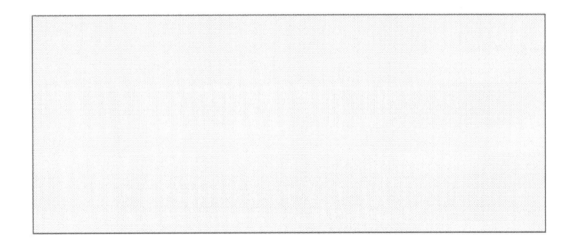

# TICKET
DIARY
# STUB

**DATE:**

## MY MEMORIES

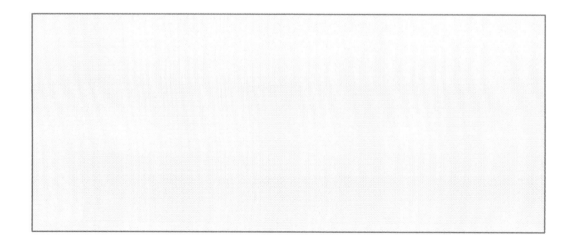

# TICKET
DIARY
# STUB

**DATE:**

## MY MEMORIES

# TICKET
DIARY
# STUB

**DATE:**

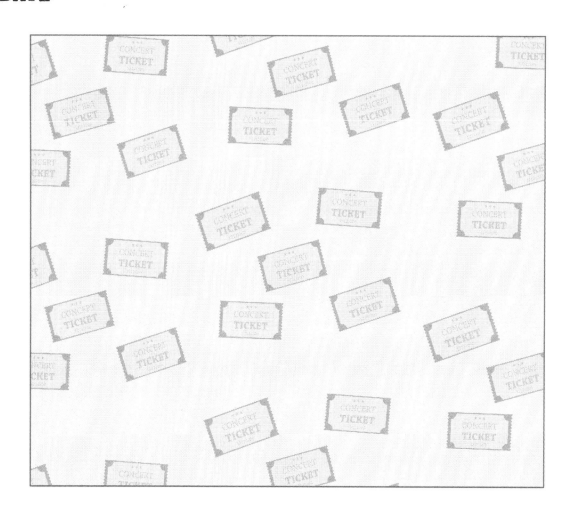

## MY MEMORIES

# TICKET
DIARY
## STUB

**DATE:**

## MY MEMORIES

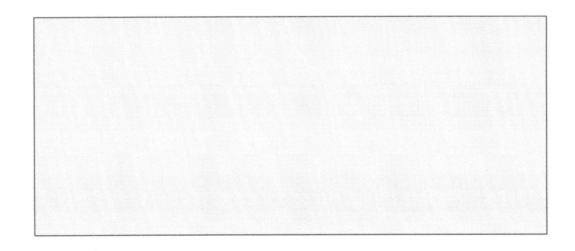

# TICKET
DIARY
# STUB

**DATE:**

## MY MEMORIES

# TICKET
DIARY
# STUB

**DATE:**

## MY MEMORIES

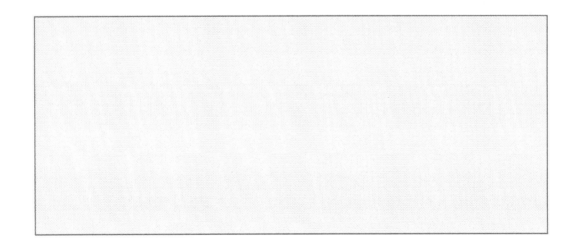

# TICKET
DIARY
# STUB

**DATE:**

## MY MEMORIES

# TICKET
DIARY
# STUB

**DATE:**

## MY MEMORIES

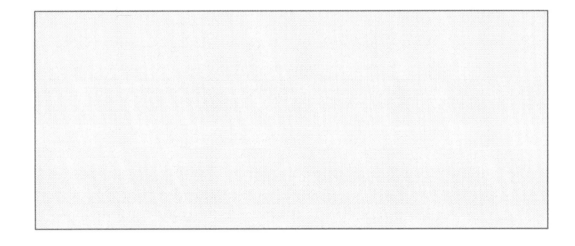

# TICKET
DIARY
# STUB

**DATE:**

## MY MEMORIES

# TICKET
DIARY
# STUB

**DATE:**

## MY MEMORIES

# TICKET
DIARY
# STUB

**DATE:**

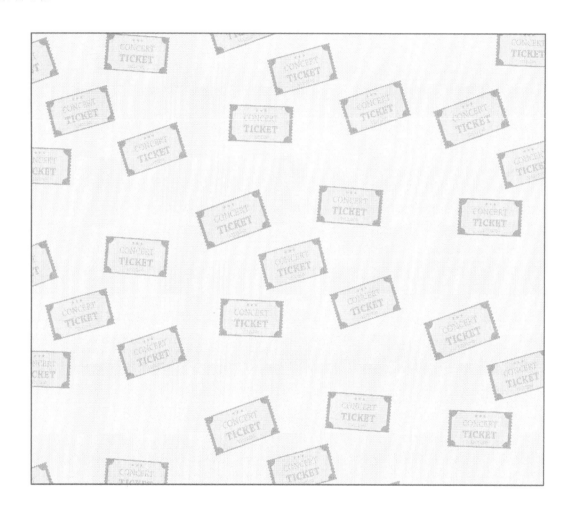

## MY MEMORIES

# TICKET
DIARY
# STUB

**DATE:**

## MY MEMORIES

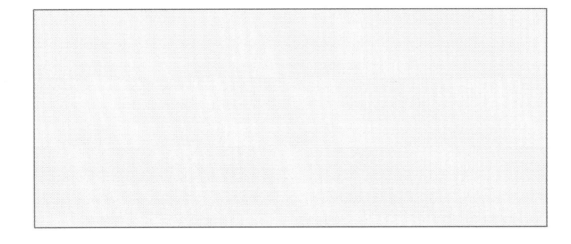

# TICKET
DIARY
# STUB

DATE:

## MY MEMORIES

# TICKET
DIARY
# STUB

**DATE:**

## MY MEMORIES

# TICKET
DIARY
# STUB

**DATE:**

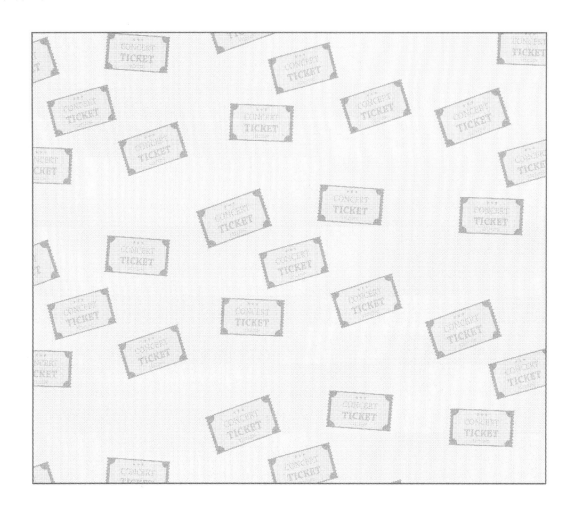

## MY MEMORIES

# TICKET
DIARY
# STUB

**DATE:**

## MY MEMORIES

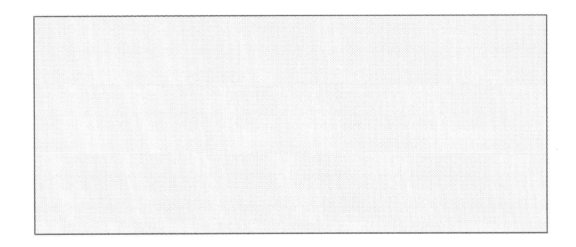

# TICKET
DIARY
# STUB

**DATE:**

## MY MEMORIES

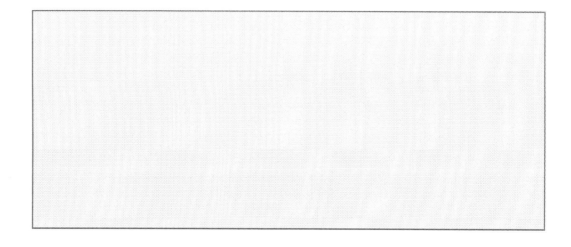

# TICKET
DIARY
# STUB

**DATE:**

**MY MEMORIES**

# TICKET
DIARY
# STUB

**DATE:**

## MY MEMORIES

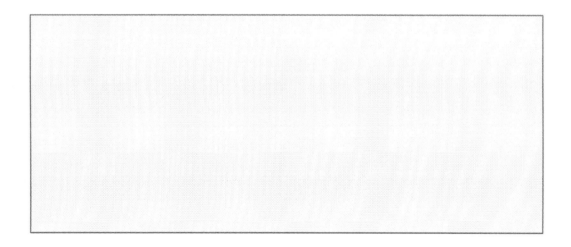

# TICKET
### DIARY
## STUB

**DATE:**

## MY MEMORIES

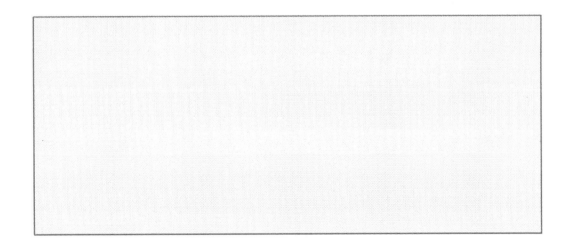

# TICKET
DIARY
# STUB

**DATE:**

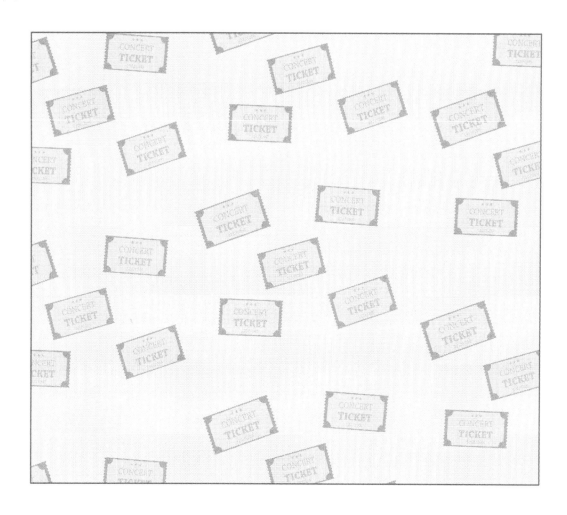

**MY MEMORIES**

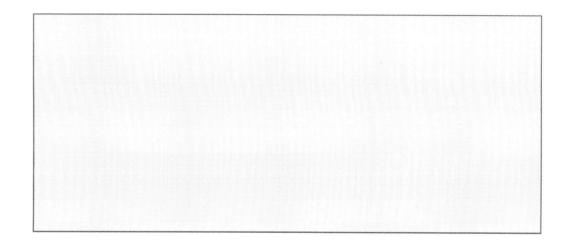

# TICKET
### DIARY
# STUB

**DATE:**

## MY MEMORIES

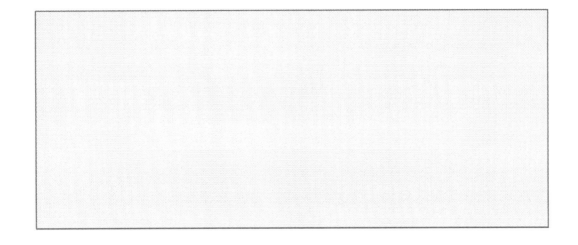

# TICKET
DIARY
# STUB

**DATE:**

## MY MEMORIES

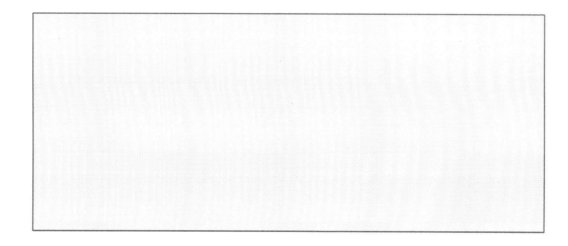

# TICKET
DIARY
# STUB

**DATE:**

## MY MEMORIES

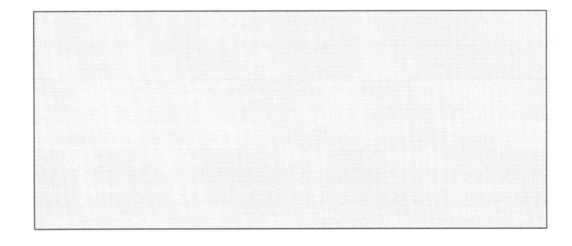

# TICKET
### DIARY
# STUB

**DATE:**

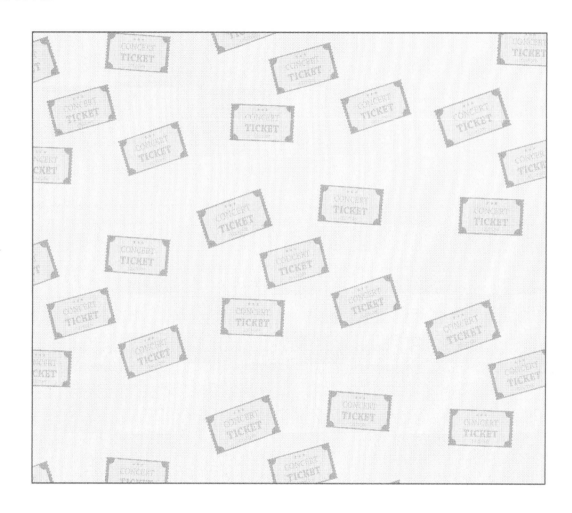

## MY MEMORIES

# TICKET
DIARY
# STUB

**DATE:**

## MY MEMORIES

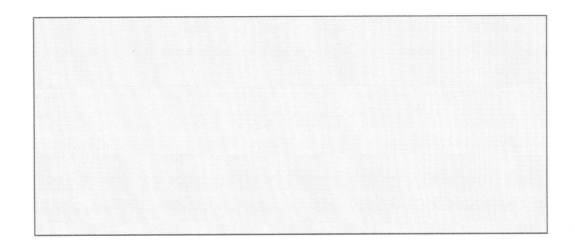

# TICKET
### DIARY
# STUB

**DATE:**

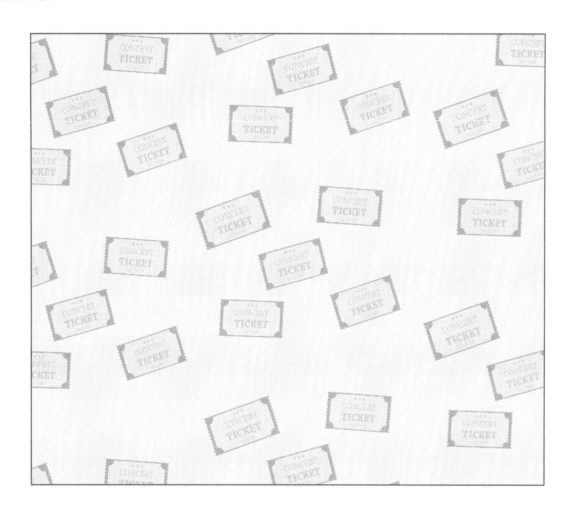

## MY MEMORIES

# TICKET
DIARY
# STUB

**DATE:**

## MY MEMORIES

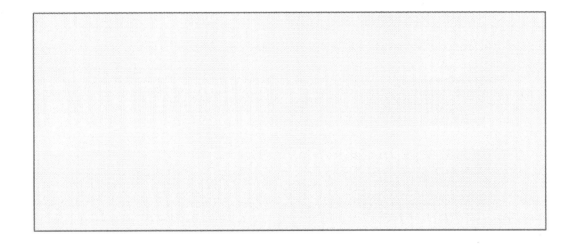

# TICKET
DIARY
## STUB

**DATE:**

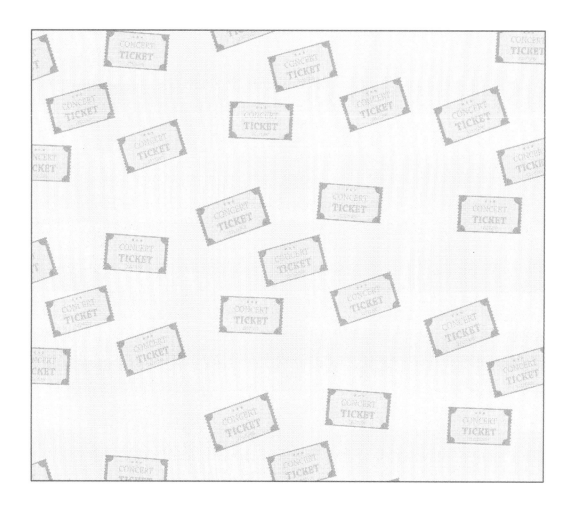

## MY MEMORIES

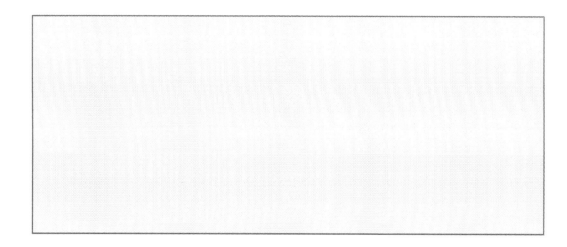

# TICKET
DIARY
# STUB

**DATE:**

**MY MEMORIES**

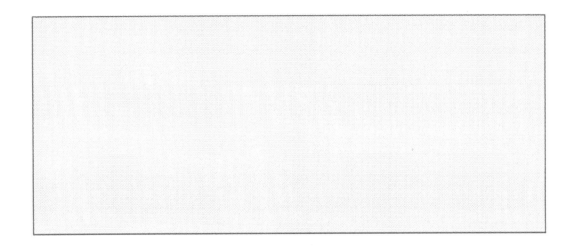

# TICKET
DIARY
# STUB

DATE:

## MY MEMORIES

# TICKET
## DIARY
# STUB

**DATE:**

## MY MEMORIES

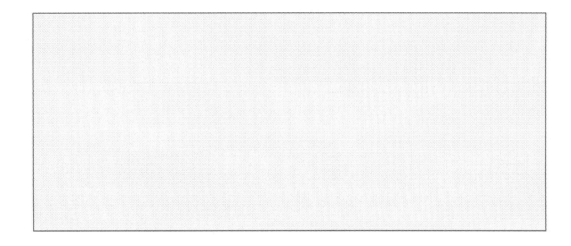

# TICKET
DIARY
# STUB

**DATE:**

## MY MEMORIES

# TICKET
DIARY
# STUB

**DATE:**

## MY MEMORIES

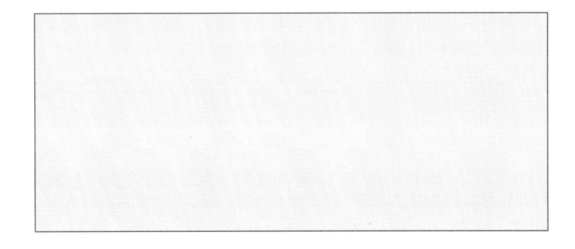

# TICKET
DIARY
# STUB

DATE:

## MY MEMORIES

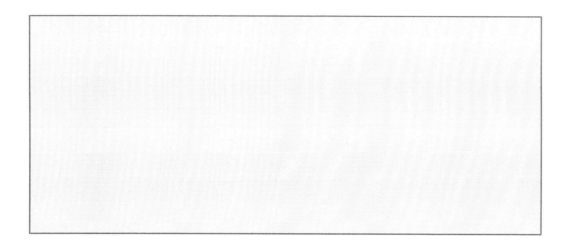

# TICKET
DIARY
# STUB

**DATE:**

## MY MEMORIES

# TICKET
DIARY
# STUB

**DATE:**

## MY MEMORIES

# TICKET
### DIARY
# STUB

**DATE:**

## MY MEMORIES

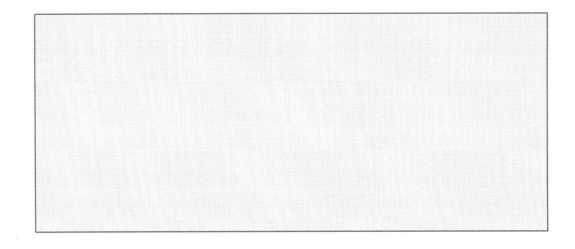

# TICKET
### DIARY
## STUB

**DATE:**

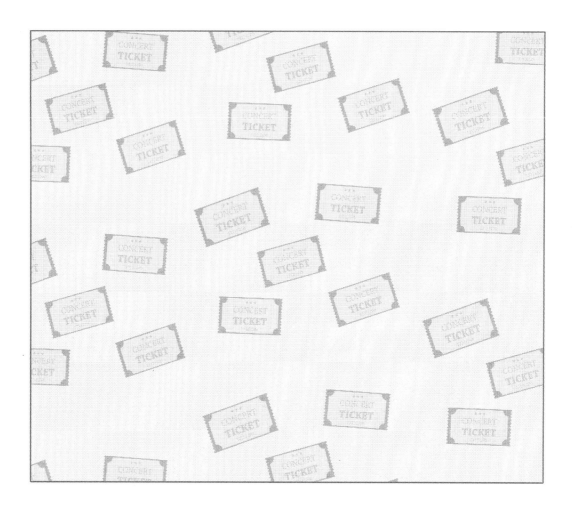

## MY MEMORIES

# TICKET
### DIARY
## STUB

**DATE:**

**MY MEMORIES**

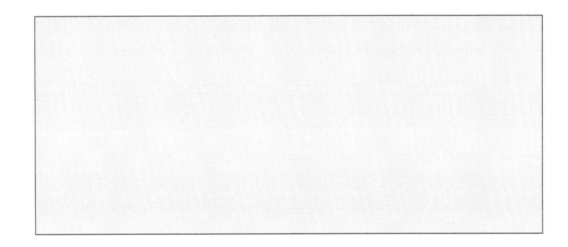

# TICKET
### DIARY
# STUB

**DATE:**

## MY MEMORIES

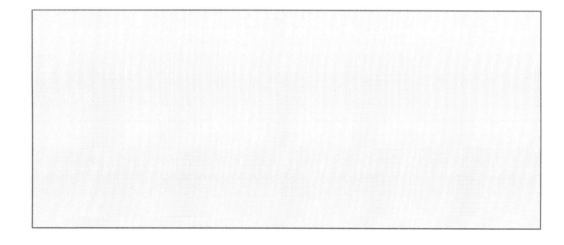

# TICKET
### DIARY
# STUB

**DATE:**

## MY MEMORIES

# TICKET
DIARY
# STUB

**DATE:**

## MY MEMORIES

# TICKET
### DIARY
## STUB

**DATE:**

**MY MEMORIES**

# TICKET
DIARY
# STUB

**DATE:**

## MY MEMORIES

# TICKET
DIARY
# STUB

**DATE:**

## MY MEMORIES

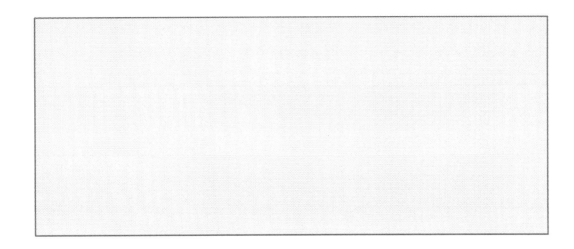

# TICKET
DIARY
# STUB

**DATE:**

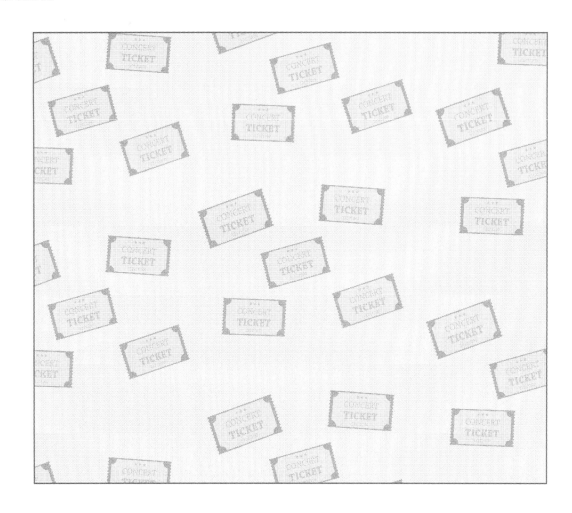

## MY MEMORIES

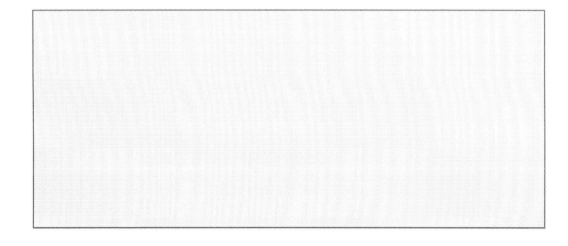

# TICKET
DIARY
# STUB

**DATE:**

**MY MEMORIES**

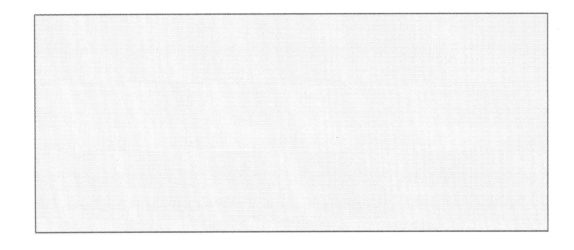

# TICKET
DIARY
## STUB

**DATE:**

## MY MEMORIES

# TICKET
DIARY
# STUB

**DATE:**

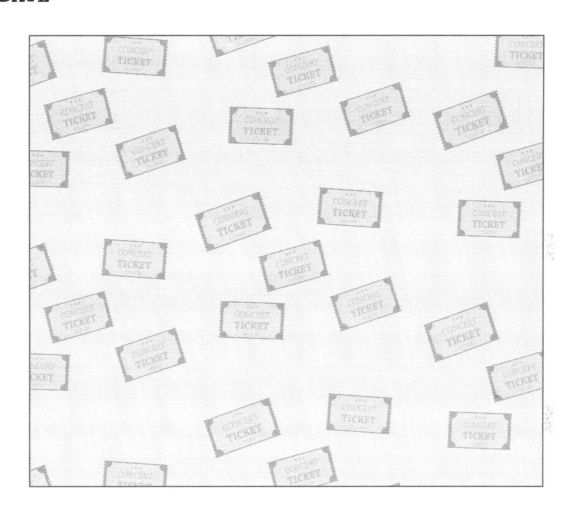

## MY MEMORIES

# TICKET
DIARY
# STUB

**DATE:**

## MY MEMORIES

# TICKET
DIARY
# STUB

**DATE:**

**MY MEMORIES**

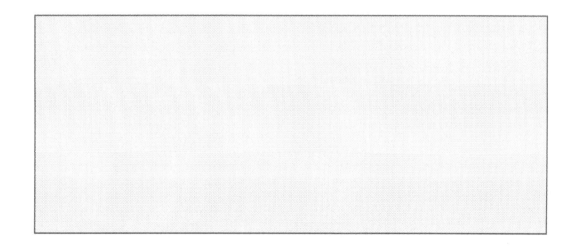

# TICKET
DIARY
# STUB

**DATE:**

## MY MEMORIES

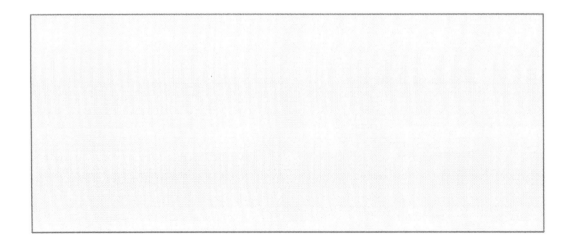

# TICKET
DIARY
# STUB

**DATE:**

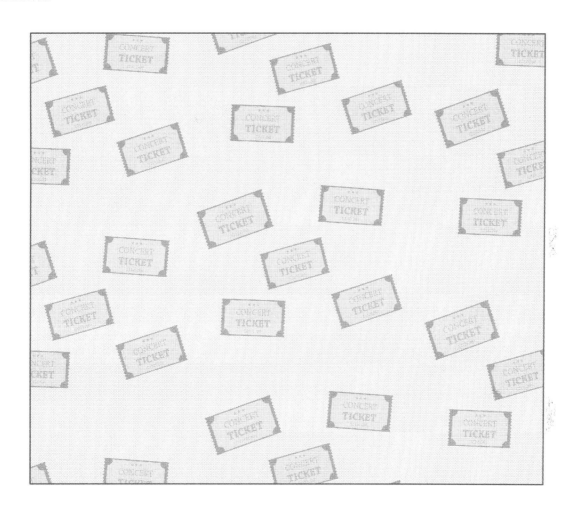

**MY MEMORIES**

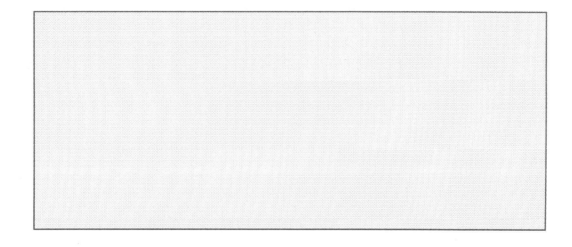

# TICKET
DIARY
# STUB

**DATE:**

**MY MEMORIES**

# TICKET
DIARY
# STUB

**DATE:**

## MY MEMORIES

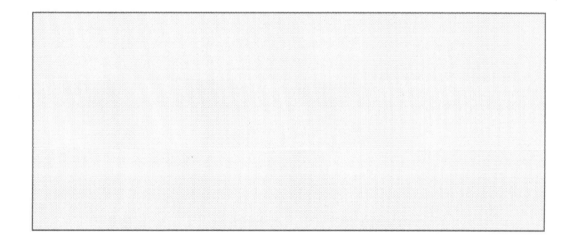

# TICKET
DIARY
## STUB

**DATE:**

## MY MEMORIES

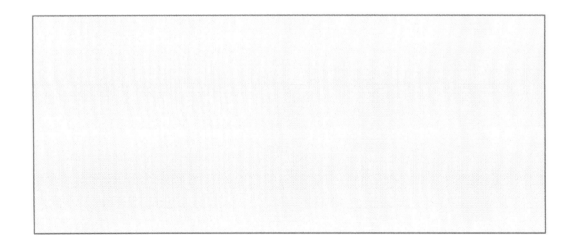

# TICKET
### DIARY
# STUB

**DATE:**

**MY MEMORIES**

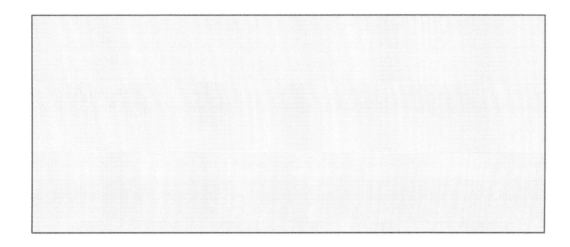

# TICKET
DIARY
# STUB

**DATE:**

## MY MEMORIES

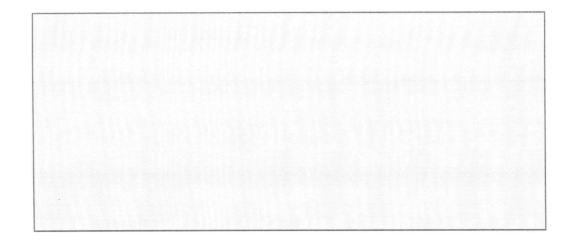

# TICKET
DIARY
# STUB

**DATE:**

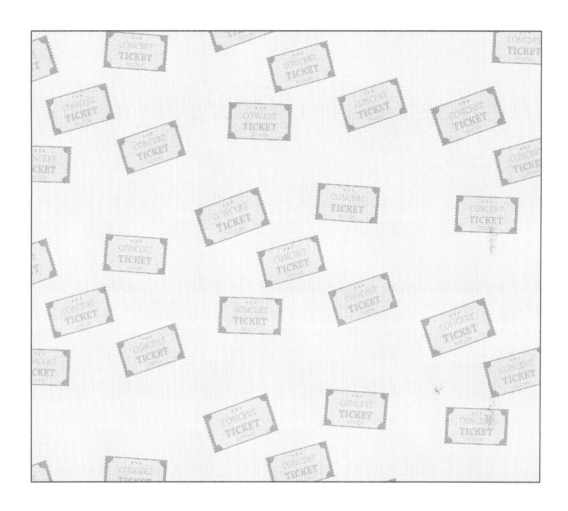

## MY MEMORIES

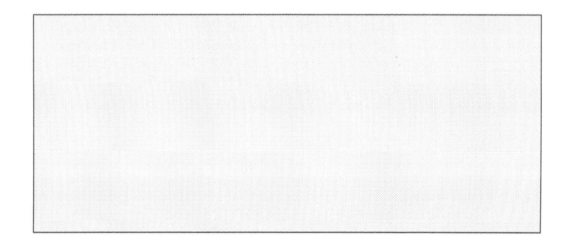

# TICKET
DIARY
# STUB

**DATE:**

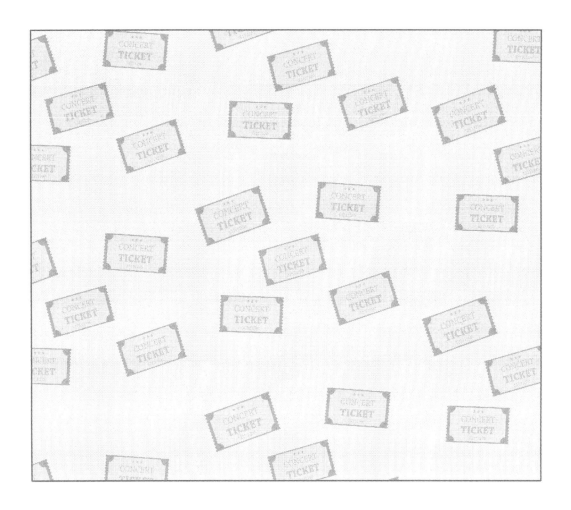

## MY MEMORIES

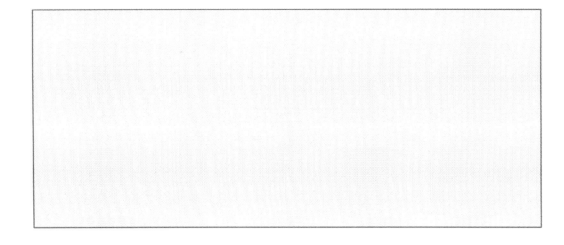

# TICKET
DIARY
# STUB

**DATE:**

**MY MEMORIES**

# TICKET
DIARY
# STUB

**DATE:**

## MY MEMORIES

# TICKET
### DIARY
# STUB

**DATE:**

**MY MEMORIES**

# TICKET
DIARY
# STUB

**DATE:**

## MY MEMORIES

# TICKET
### DIARY
# STUB

**DATE:**

**MY MEMORIES**

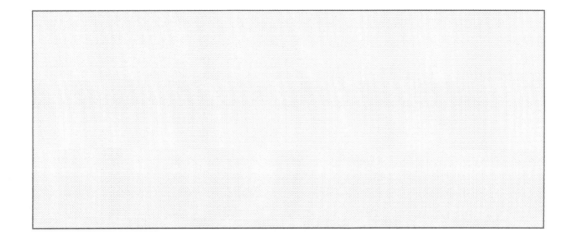

# TICKET
DIARY
# STUB

**DATE:**

## MY MEMORIES

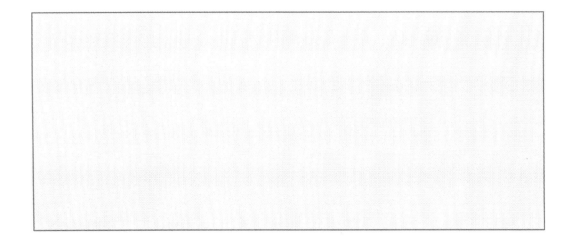

# TICKET
### DIARY
# STUB

**DATE:**

**MY MEMORIES**

# TICKET
DIARY
# STUB

**DATE:**

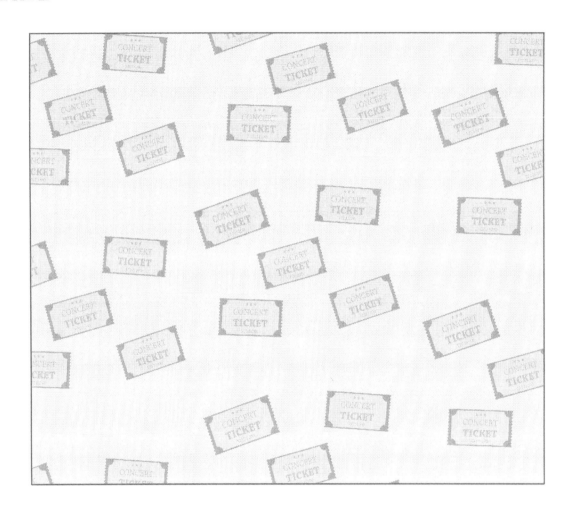

## MY MEMORIES

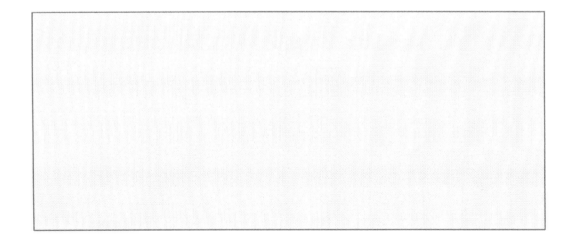

# TICKET
### DIARY
# STUB

**DATE:**

## MY MEMORIES

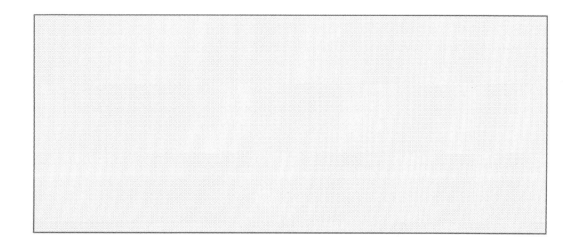

# TICKET
### DIARY
# STUB

**DATE:**

## MY MEMORIES

# TICKET
### DIARY
# STUB

**DATE:**

**MY MEMORIES**

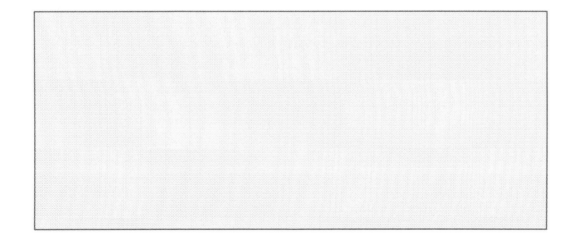

# TICKET
DIARY
# STUB

**DATE:**

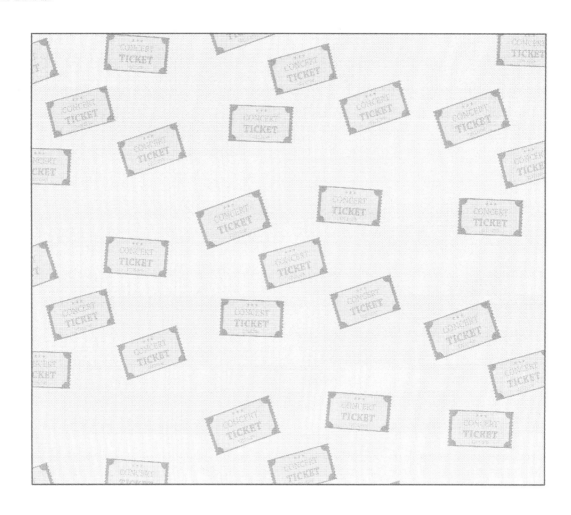

## MY MEMORIES

# TICKET
DIARY
# STUB

**DATE:**

## MY MEMORIES

# TICKET
### DIARY
# STUB

**DATE:**

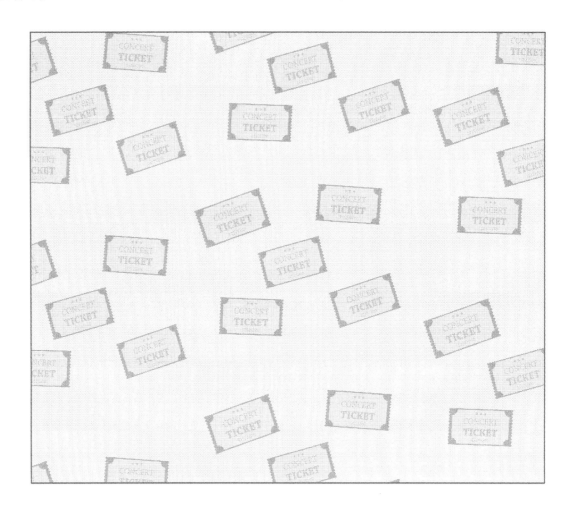

## MY MEMORIES

# TICKET
DIARY
# STUB

**DATE:**

**MY MEMORIES**

# TICKET
DIARY
# STUB

**DATE:**

**MY MEMORIES**

# TICKET
## DIARY
# STUB

**DATE:**

**MY MEMORIES**

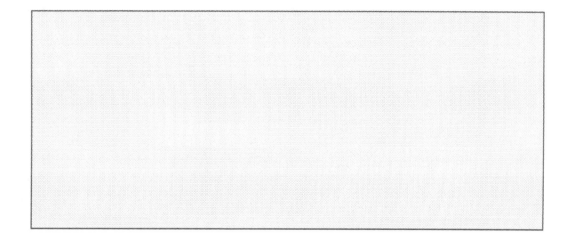

# TICKET
DIARY
# STUB

**DATE:**

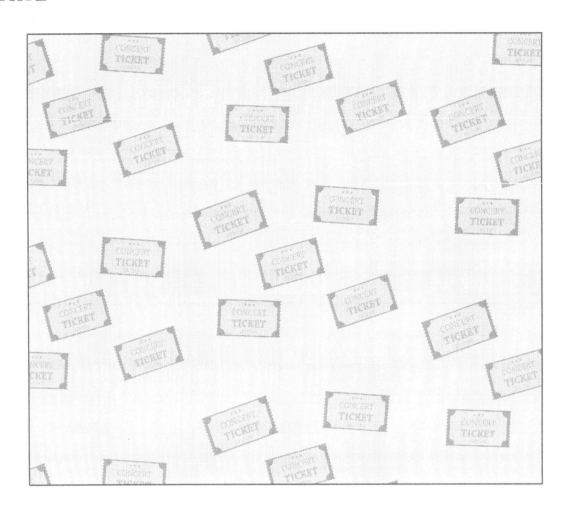

**MY MEMORIES**

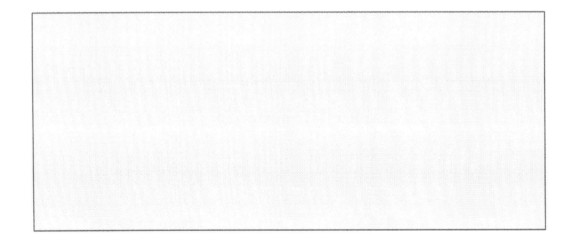

# TICKET
DIARY
# STUB

**DATE:**

**MY MEMORIES**

# TICKET
DIARY
# STUB

**DATE:**

## MY MEMORIES

# TICKET
DIARY
# STUB

**DATE:**

## MY MEMORIES

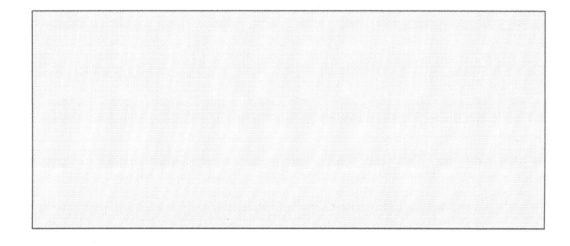

# TICKET
DIARY
# STUB

DATE:

## MY MEMORIES

# TICKET
DIARY
# STUB

**DATE:**

## MY MEMORIES

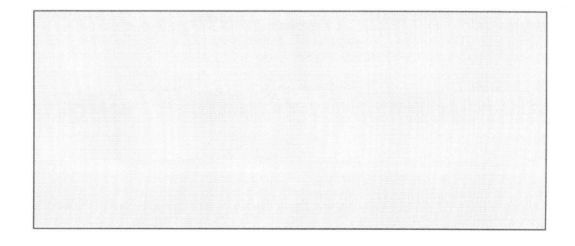

# TICKET
DIARY
# STUB

**DATE:**

**MY MEMORIES**

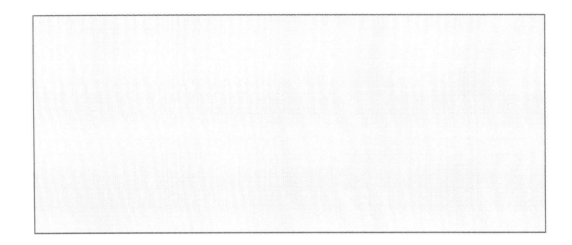

# TICKET
### DIARY
# STUB

**DATE:**

**MY MEMORIES**

# TICKET
DIARY
# STUB

**DATE:**

## MY MEMORIES

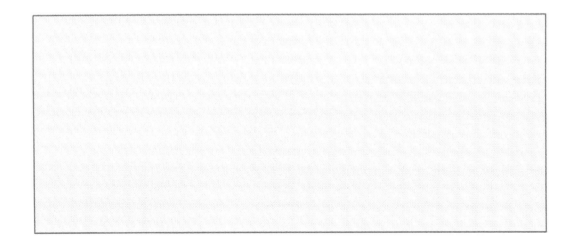

# TICKET
DIARY
# STUB

**DATE**:

**MY MEMORIES**

# TICKET
DIARY
# STUB

**DATE:**

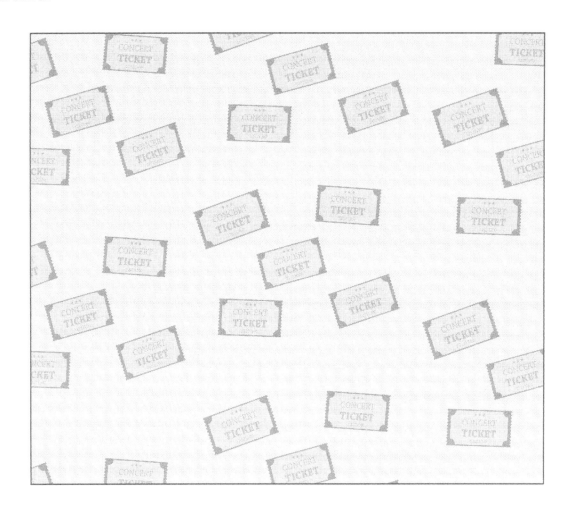

## MY MEMORIES

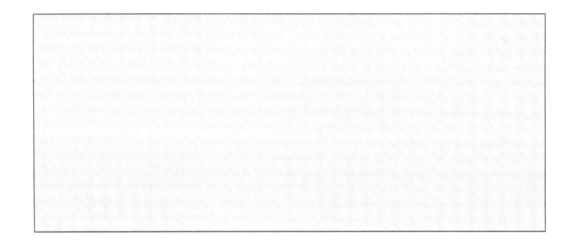

# TICKET
### DIARY
# STUB

**DATE:**

**MY MEMORIES**

# TICKET
DIARY
# STUB

**DATE:**

## MY MEMORIES

# TICKET
### DIARY
# STUB

**DATE:**

**MY MEMORIES**

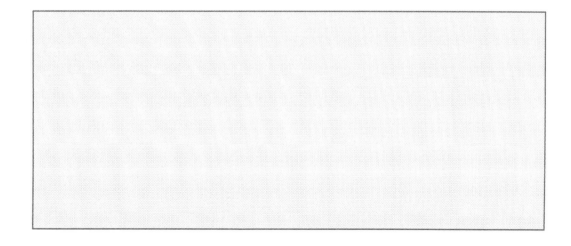

# TICKET
DIARY
# STUB

**DATE:**

## MY MEMORIES

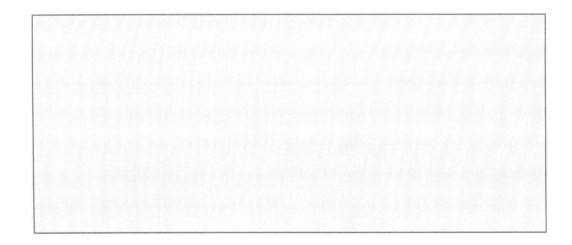

# TICKET
### DIARY
# STUB

**DATE:**

## MY MEMORIES

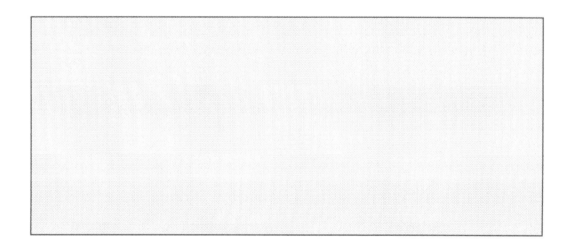

# TICKET
DIARY
# STUB

**DATE:**

## MY MEMORIES

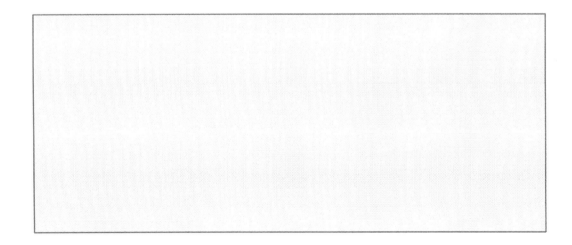

# TICKET
DIARY
# STUB

**DATE:**

**MY MEMORIES**

# TICKET
DIARY
## STUB

**DATE:**

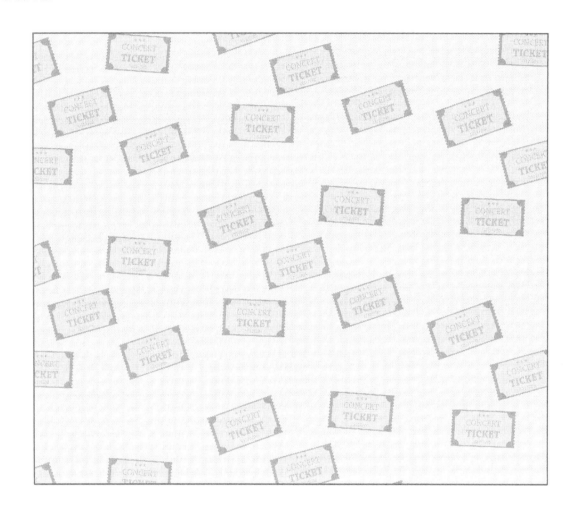

## MY MEMORIES

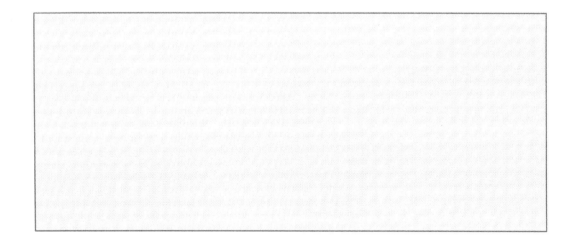

# TICKET
### DIARY
# STUB

**DATE:**

**MY MEMORIES**

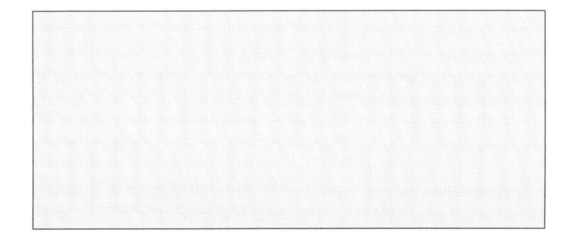

# TICKET
DIARY
# STUB

**DATE:**

## MY MEMORIES

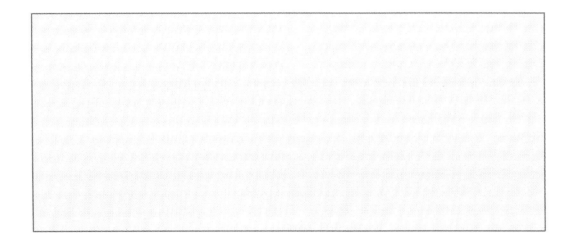

# TICKET
DIARY
# STUB

**DATE:**

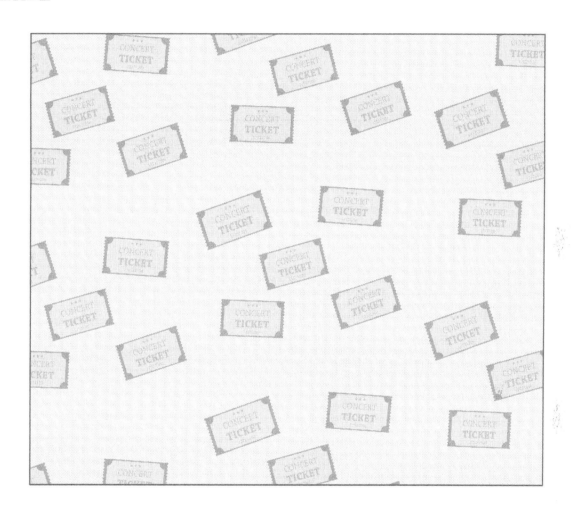

## MY MEMORIES

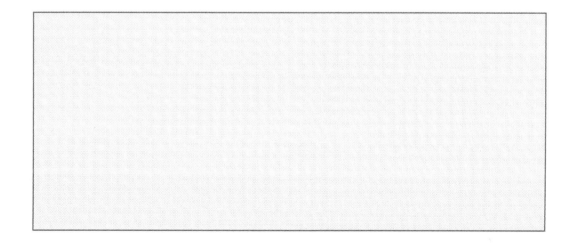

# TICKET
DIARY
# STUB

**DATE:**

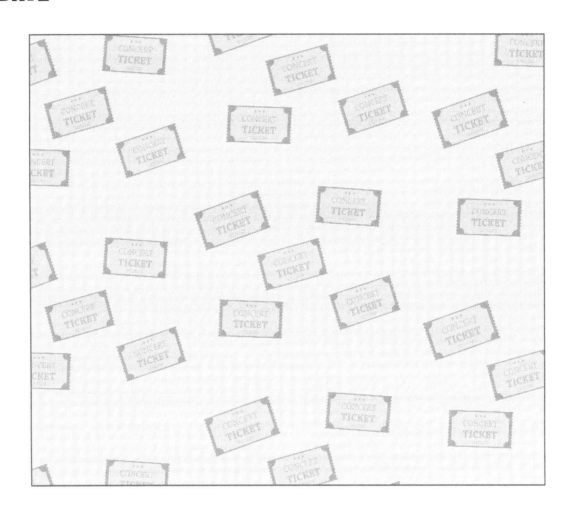

## MY MEMORIES

# TICKET
DIARY
# STUB

**DATE:**

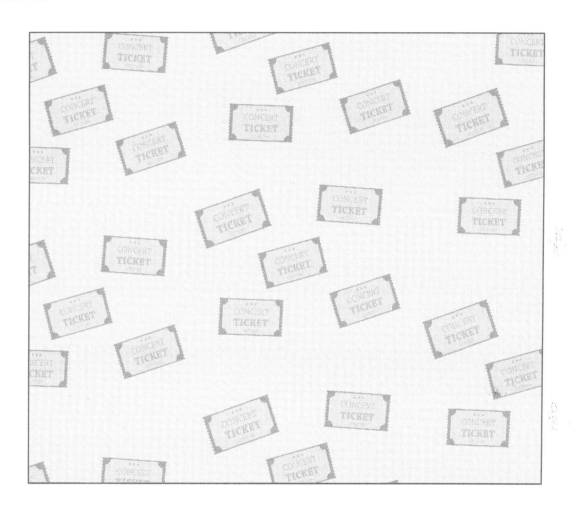

**MY MEMORIES**

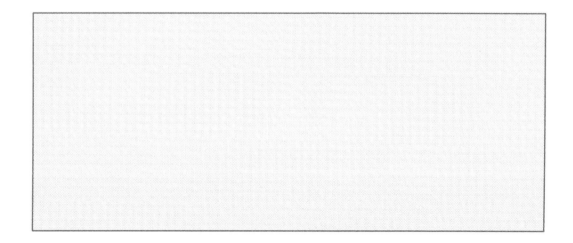

# TICKET
DIARY
# STUB

**DATE:**

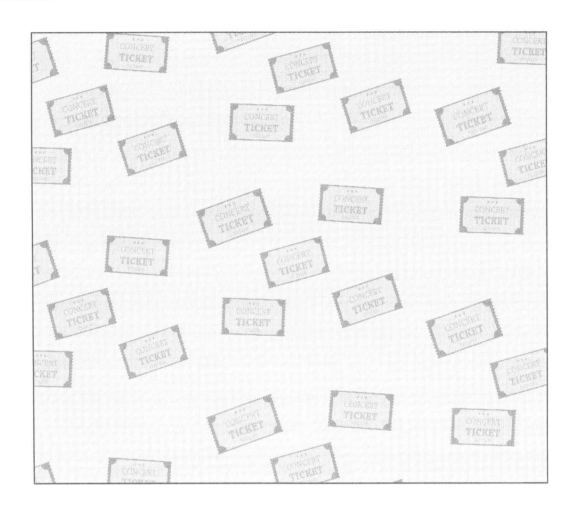

## MY MEMORIES

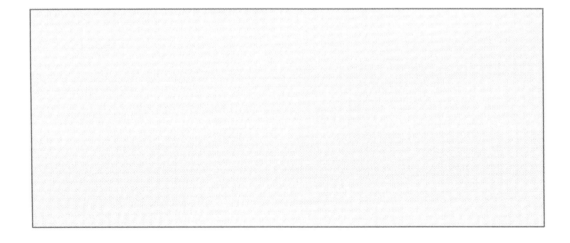

# TICKET
## DIARY
# STUB

**DATE:**

## MY MEMORIES

# TICKET
DIARY
# STUB

**DATE:**

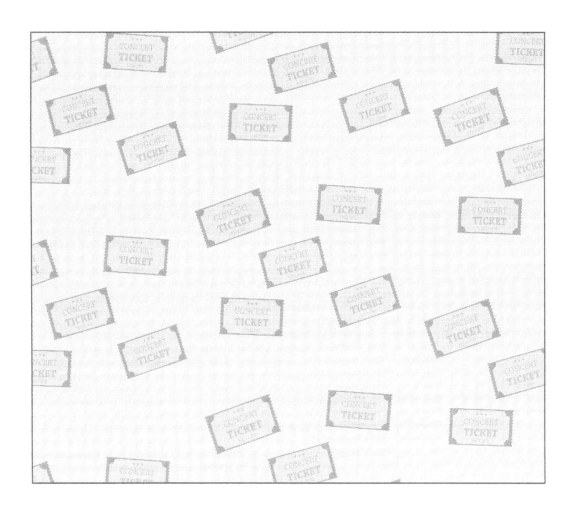

## MY MEMORIES

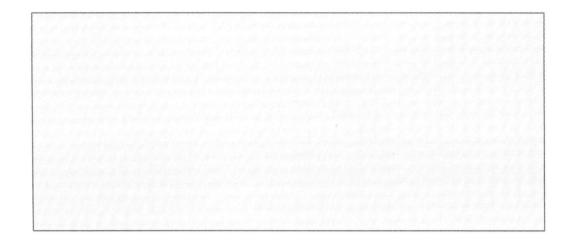

# TICKET
### DIARY
# STUB

**DATE:**

## MY MEMORIES

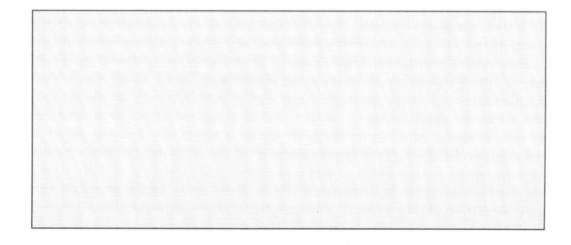

# TICKET
DIARY
# STUB

**DATE:**

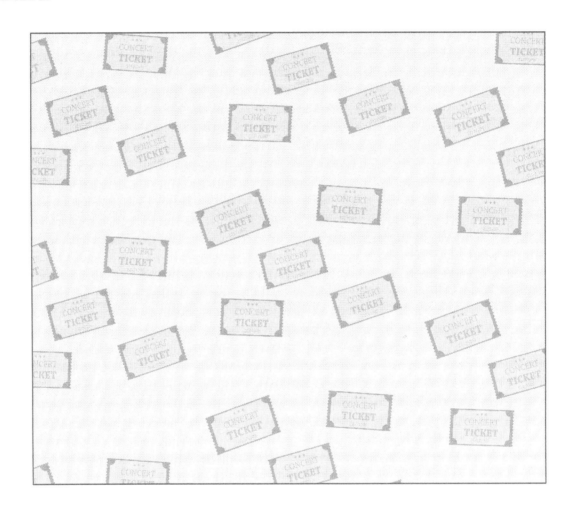

## MY MEMORIES

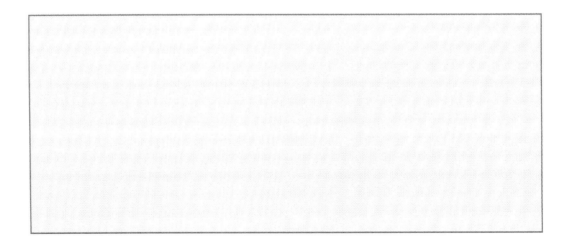

# TICKET
DIARY
# STUB

**DATE:**

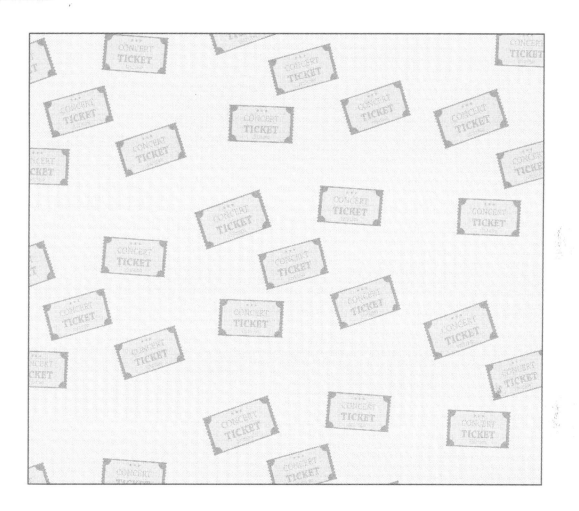

## MY MEMORIES

# TICKET
DIARY
# STUB

**DATE:**

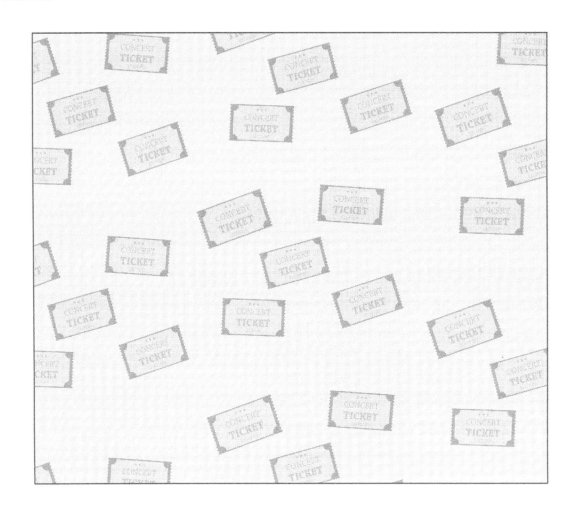

## MY MEMORIES

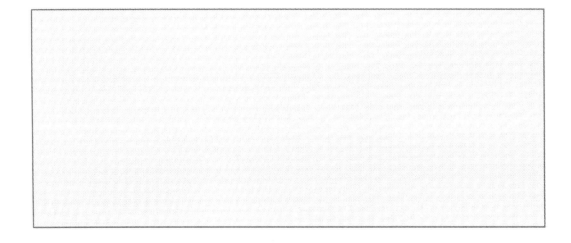

# TICKET
DIARY
# STUB

**DATE:**

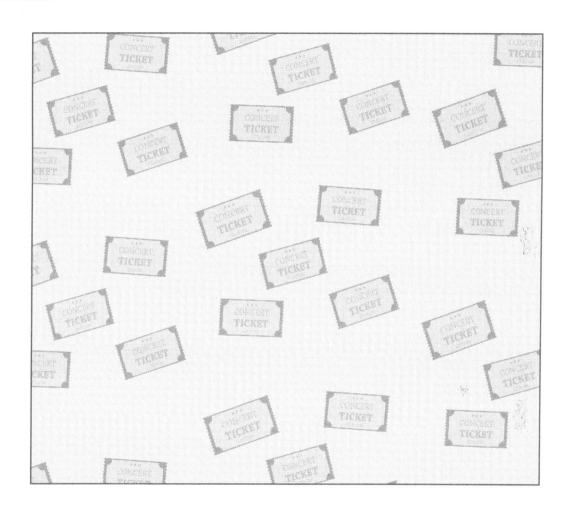

## MY MEMORIES

# TICKET
DIARY
# STUB

**DATE:**

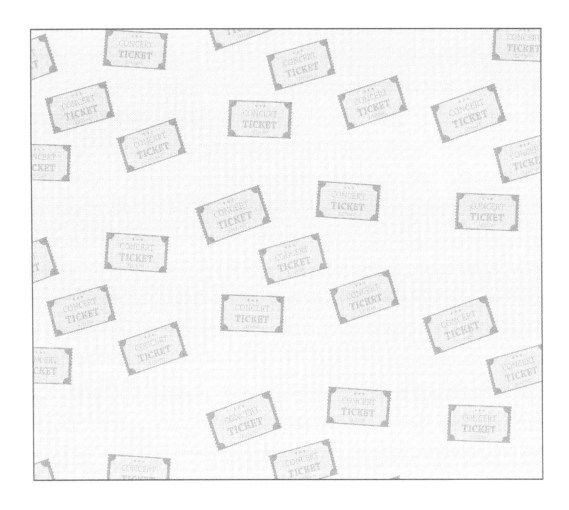

## MY MEMORIES

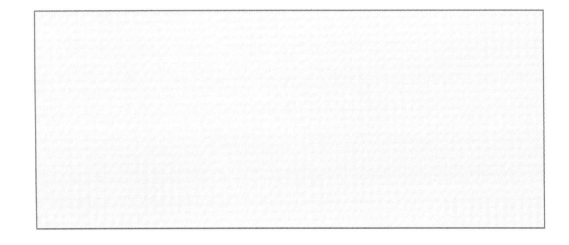

# TICKET
### DIARY
# STUB

**DATE:**

## MY MEMORIES

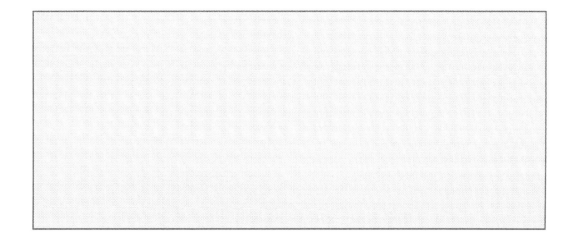

# TICKET
DIARY
# STUB

**DATE:**

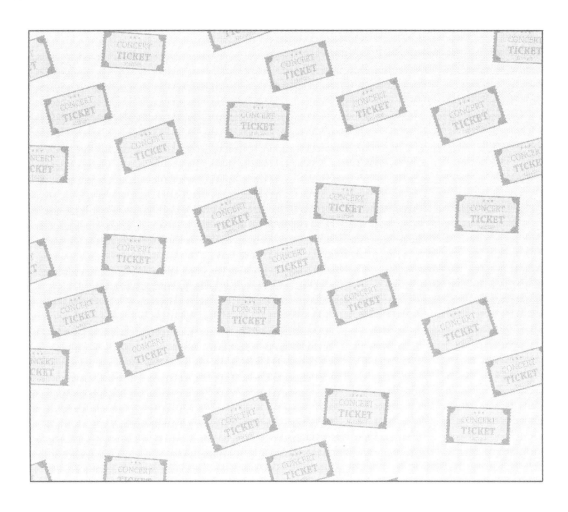

**MY MEMORIES**

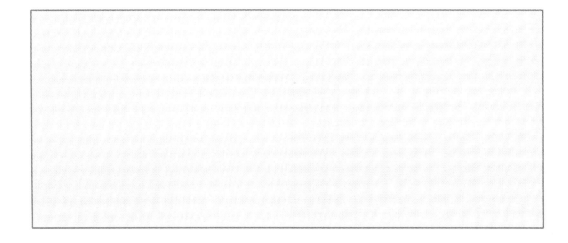

Printed in Great Britain
by Amazon